CANS
STUART SLADE

Cans was first produced by Theatre503, London, in association with
Kuleshov on 4 November 2014

CANS
STUART SLADE

CAST

Uncle Len	Graham O'Mara
Jen	Jennifer Clement

CREATIVE TEAM

Director	Dan Pick
Producers	Lucy Hollis & Ruth Milne
	(in association with Etch)
Production Manager	Holly Hooper
Production Design	Georgia de Grey
Lighting Design	Christopher Nairne
Marketing Design	Lucy Newman, Neni Almeida
Sound Design	Kieran Lucas
Composer	Ned Roberts
PR	Chloe Nelkin Consulting
Artistic Director at Theatre503	Paul Robinson
Head of Marketing at Theatre503	Polly Ingham
Associate Artistic Director at Theatre503	Lisa Cagnacci
Literary Manager at Theatre503	Steve Harper

kuleshov

Kuleshov is a theatre company committed to developing innovative and powerful new writing. We have three Artistic Directors – Dan Pick, Stuart Slade and Graham O'Mara.

Cans is produced in association with Lucy Hollis & Ruth Milne of Etch.

www.kuleshov.co.uk

e___tch

Etch is a brand new theatre company focusing on new writing. We aim to discover, nurture and support new work whilst encouraging collaboration amongst emerging artists. Through our monthly scratch nights at The Peckham Pelican we provide a base and a platform for development and discussion, creating a fluid community where artists can connect and make work.

www.etchtheatre.com

THEATRE 503

Theatre503 is the award-winning home of groundbreaking plays.

Led by Artistic Director Paul Robinson, Theatre503 is a flagship fringe venue committed to producing new work that is game-changing, relevant, surprising, mischievous, visually thrilling and theatrical. Our theatre is one of London's few destinations for new writing and we offer more opportunities to new writers than any other theatre in the country.

THEATRE503 TEAM

Artistic Director	Paul Robinson
Executive Director	Jeremy Woodhouse
Producer and Head of Marketing	Polly Ingham
Associate Artistic Director	Lisa Cagnacci
Development Director	Caroline Downing
Office Manager	Joe Brown
Literary Manager	Steve Harper
Literary Coordinators	Lauretta Barrow, Tom Latter
Literary Associate	Karis Halsall
Resident Assistant Producers	Hattie Callery, Emily Hubert
Senior Readers	Kate Brower, Clare O'Hara, Jimmy Osbourne, Imogen Sarre
Associate Directors	James Dacre, Gemma Fairlie, Tom Littler
Associate Artist	Johanna Towne

THEATRE503 BOARD

And we couldn't do what we do without our brilliant volunteers:

Annabel Pemberton, Nuno Faisca, Rosie Akerman, Diyan Zora, Tobias Chapple, Joseph Ackerman, Alexandra Coyne, Anuska Zaremba-Pike, Cecilia Segar, Valeria Bello, Larner Taylor, Damian Robertson, Jumoke, Valeria Carboni, Mike Bale, Serafina Cusack, Louise Fairbrother, Caroline Jowett, Jim Mannering, Oluwafuntu Ojumu, Imogen Robertson, Chidimma Chukwu, Jill Segal, Elena Valentine, Tess Hardy, Kenneth Hawes, Anna Gorajek, Maya Kirtley.

Theatre503 is supported by:

Angela Hyde-Courtney and the Audience Club, Kay Ellen Consolver, Cas Donald, Edna Kissman, Eileen Glynn, Deborah Shaw and Steve Marqhardt, Marisa Drew, Jerwood/Ponsonby, Andrew and Julia Johnson, Georgia Oetker, Stuart Mullins, Michael Morfey, Geraldine Sharpe-Newton, Penny Egan, Liz Padmore, Bernice Chitnis, Lisa Forrell, Abigail Thaw, Charlotte Westenra, Frankie Sangwin, Mike and Hilary Tyler, Sue and Keith Hamilton, Sandra Chalmers, David Chapman and Judy Molloy, Georgie Grant Haworth, Amy Rotherham, Kate Beswick, Craig Simpson, Jason Meiniger, Yve Newbold, Philip and Chris Carne, Juliana Breitenbach.

Theatre503, 503 Battersea Park Rd, London SW11 3BW
020 7978 7040 I www.theatre503.com
@Theatre503 I Facebook.com/theatre503

Shine a light on Theatre503...

Theatre503 receives no public subsidy as a venue and we cannot survive without the transformative support of our friends. For as little as £23 a year you can help us remain 'Arguably the most important theatre in Britain today' (*Guardian*).

Becoming a Friend of Theatre503 is simple.
Annual support donations are invited in five tiers:

FOOTLIGHT
£23
- Priority notice of productions and events
- Priority booking for all productions
- Special ticket offers
- Email bulletins

SPOTLIGHT
£53
As Footlight, plus:
- Access to sold-out shows
- Credit in the theatre foyer, playtexts, and on the website

LIMELIGHT
£173
As Spotlight, plus:
- Two complimentary tickets to Theatre503's hottest new play each year
- Complimentary tickets to play readings and other one-off supporter events
- Free programmes
- Ticket exchange service for pre-booked tickets (with twenty-four hours' notice)

HIGHLIGHT
£503
As Limelight, plus:
- Two complimentary tickets for each Theatre503 in-house production
- Opportunities to attend rehearsals
- Invitation to annual high-level supporters' party hosted by the Artistic Director

STARLIGHT
£1003
A bespoke package enables our Starlight to engage with Theatre503's work as they wish. This can include bespoke entertaining opportunities at the theatre, invitations to attend supper parties with the Artistic Director, or closer engagement with playwrights and the artistic team. Starlights can also choose a strand of Theatre503's work to support, for example a particular production, funding Theatre503 writing programmes or work in the local community. Please visit our website theatre503.com for details on specific appeals also.

One off donations also make an enormous difference to the way Theatre503 is able to operate. Whether you are able to give £10 or £1000 your gift will help us continue to create work of award-winning standard.

To become a member or make a one off donation email your interest to: **info@theatre503.com**, or by post to: Theatre503, The Latchmere, 503 Battersea Park Road, London, SW11 3BW.

Alternatively visit our website **theatre503.com** or ring **020 7978 7040** to sign up for membership directly.

If you are a UK tax payer and able to make a gift aid donation please let us know as we receive 25p per pound more on top of your donation in government grant.

CANS

Stuart Slade

Characters

UNCLE LEN, *forties*

JEN, *twenties*

Scenes

Each scene takes place about a month after the previous scene.

This text went to press before the end of rehearsals and so may differ slightly from the play as performed.

1. Of Mice and Jen

The inside of a domestic garage. No car, but the walls lined with shelves of junk.

Two chairs. LEN *enters, carrying a bucket of water.* JEN *follows, carrying a tote bag very gingerly.*

JEN (*already lost the battle*). This is *utterly* skanky, alright?

LEN *doesn't reply.*

It's… evil and twisted and just *wrong* on so many levels. I'm just – I'm just *not* –

LEN (*without rancour*). Didn't ask for no help.

LEN *sits down and invites* JEN *to do the same.*

JEN. No.

He gestures again.

No.

LEN (*through a cough*). Bender.

JEN. Come the fuck on, Uncle Len.

LEN *pulls a can of cider from each pocket.*

LEN (*genially*). Can of cider? Make it more of a *thing*?

JEN. A *thing*? Jesus.

LEN *passes a can of cider to* JEN. LEN *opens his cider. Pause.*

(*Pointing to the bucket.*) Is it *warm* water at least?

LEN. No it's not *warm* water, you great spastic. We're drowning the cunts, not treating them to an invigorating fucking spa weekend.

JEN. I just think drowning them in warm water would be… nicer. That's all.

JEN *opens her can of cider.*

LEN (*rolling his eyes*). *Nicer?* Fucking give 'em a makeover first, if you want. Read them some poetry.

LEN *gestures for* JEN *to sit down. Eventually she does, with a sigh.*

JEN. I don't see why we just can't drive into the countryside –

(*Points at the bag.*) Set the poor things free.

LEN. Be back here like a fucking shot.

JEN. They're fucking *mice*, Uncle Len, not like – homing pigeons.

LEN (*shrugs*). Telling you.

JEN. Are they furry little fucking experts in orienteering, Uncle Len? Have they got little tiny maps and compasses? Have they fuck.

LEN. Should have bought the snap traps, like I told you.

JEN. No – they're fucking rough as.

LEN (*parodic effeminate voice*). *Humane* traps?

(*Shakes his head.*) What you going to do with them once you caught 'em? Take 'em to dinner? Fuck 'em?

(*Smiles.*) Seriously, though – my mate Shaun, right, plagued by the fuckers – got humane traps, right, because his wife was like this – (*Mimes mouth yapping into his ear with his hand.*) he throws one into a hedge, right, five miles from home. Cunt was back the next day, with a face like this – (*Mimes angry face.*)

JEN. It clearly wasn't the same mouse, was it?

LEN. Jen. The mouse was all like: 'I seen some crazy shit, man, and now I'm going to Fuck. You. Up.' Shat in his cereal box next morning, didn't notice it, ate it, got fucking mice-shit AIDS. Never been the fucking same.

JEN. That's utter balls.

LEN. Come on, mate. Suck it up. Game face on.

JEN. We can't do this. Uncle Len. We just can't.

Pause.

LEN. You going to do the first one, or am I?

JEN. *No.* No.

LEN. Right then.

LEN *picks a small perspex box and a stick from the tote bag. He holds the box over the bucket. Ready to drop –*

JEN. Shouldn't we at least say something? Sorry or something.

Pause. LEN *holds up his can.*

LEN. Cheers!

LEN *puts the box in the water and pushes it to the bottom with the stick.*

JEN. Fuck. Fuck.

JEN *stands up, walks in a circle. She finds this extremely traumatic.*

Get him out of there, Uncle Len. Please.

LEN. Look, Jen, we got to. If you poison 'em, they crawl between the walls and die and stink up the house for months.

JEN. Len, *please*!

LEN. If you use a snap trap, you get blood and guts and shit all over your carpets – and they scream and that, like this – (*Does impression of scream.*) This way's kinder.

JEN. It's not *kind*, alright?

LEN. I know what I'm talking about, alright. I done mice, I done rats, I done foxes and next week I'm starting on badgers. Karmically I'm fucked, but I'm a fucking pro at vermin, right?

(*With something like glee.*) Look at the little bastard –
fucking going for it now. Come on, swim, you little fucker!

JEN. Stop it.

LEN. They're smaller when they're wet.

(*Philosophically.*) Fur bulks 'em out, you see. You ever seen
a cat come out a swimming pool? Look all fucking thin and
emaciated and Auschwitz-y. Fucking unsettling, a wet cat.

JEN *looks in the bucket and winces.*

JEN. This is fucking ghoulish.

LEN (*emphatically*). I promised your mum. Least I can do.

JEN. Uncle Len.

Pause.

He's not – is he?

LEN. Takes a while yet.

Horrible pause.

Nice to finally spend some time with you, Jen.

JEN. Fuck off!

LEN. Haven't seen you since… well.

(*Smiles.*) Remember, though – when we used to play Hungry
Hungry Hippo together, when you was little – used to go
mental for it – remember?

JEN (*a little fondly*). Yeah –

(*Remembering what's happening.*) and here we both are,
executing mice. Zip-a-dee-fucking-doo-dah.

LEN *points into the bucket.*

LEN. Look at the bugger now! Break-dance, Mickey! Have it
large. Boom shakalaka! Boom shakalaka!

LEN *mimes a dance.*

Nah, he's gone.

(*Does the sign of a cross.*) Ashes to ashes, dust to dust.

(*Faux-weeping*.) He's going to a better place, Jen. Well, the bin.

They're both suddenly very deflated. JEN *sits back down next to* LEN.

LEN *pulls the perspex box out of the bucket, pulls a plastic bag out of his pocket, and puts the box into it. He's careful not to get water on anything.*

Right – one down, two to go. Your go.

JEN. You must be *joking*.

LEN (*to the mouse in the box,* Goodfellas *voice*). We've whacked Mickey, now it's your turn, Minnie.

JEN *looks away.*

JEN. You can't give them names.

LEN. Why?

JEN. You just can't. It makes it... (*Shrugs*.)

LEN. Bath time, love.

LEN *puts the second perspex box into the bucket.* JEN *winces.*

She's bigger than Mickey. Do you think she'll take longer?

JEN. I've no idea.

(*Interest piqued*.) Maybe.

LEN. We should've timed the first one. Could have taken bets on it.

JEN. Fuck, Uncle Len. Can't we treat this with a bit of fucking *decorum*?

LEN. Can't let your mum down, can we?

JEN. She'd be going *mental*. If she saw this.

LEN. That's exactly the fucking problem, isn't it?

(*Realised what he's said*.) Sorry.

JEN. That's alright.

LEN. Your mum phoned me up, right, in hysterics down the fucking phone – fuck, she's trying to undo the clasp on the box –

(Pokes inside the bucket with a stick.) Hands off, Houdini.

JEN. Uncle Len.

LEN. I didn't know what to fucking say. Since your dad died –

JEN. I know. I *know*.

LEN *(very seriously)*. Said she's not been able to sleep a fucking wink.

JEN. Nor have I.

LEN. She was going on and on about the scratching, by her bed –

JEN. I know, Uncle Len.

LEN. She wasn't making any sense.

JEN. I know, alright?

Long silence.

She's stopped fighting now. The mouse –

LEN. Yeah. Poor little sod.

Pause.

You know what, right? This is exactly what it must be like for God, right, if there is one – looking down from on high – dealing out cancer and car crashes and earthquakes and stuff, relentlessly fucking people's shit up.

(Pokes inside the bucket with a stick.) He's probably up there drinking cider and all. Dirty fucking cunt.

JEN. I know.

LEN. At least we're doing this for a reason. What the fuck reason was there for your dad?

JEN. Len.

LEN. No fucker showed him fuck-all mercy, did they?

JEN. Len.

LEN. Was it *fair*, Jen? What happened to him?

JEN. Of course it wasn't.

LEN. Then why the fuck should I be any fucking different?

They look at the bucket. LEN takes the box out, puts it in the bag with the other.

Long pause.

Last one.

JEN. Uncle Len – let's not. Come on.

LEN. I owe it to your mother, Jen. We've not always seen eye to eye, but I don't want her going fucking raving on you, do I?

JEN. She won't – I mean –

LEN. Course not.

Long pause.

Look, mate. You know that I'm sorry I didn't come round here for the last month, right?

JEN. That's alright, Uncle Len.

LEN. I just completely spun out, you know? Sitting in the pub for days on end, shitfaced, fucking tears running down my fucking face. In a mess. Not taking care of myself.

JEN. I heard. It wasn't easy for anyone.

LEN. And now, right, it's the least I can do – and I mean the *very* least – to do this for him. Stop your mum from –

JEN (*interrupting*). Do you know what actually happens? Uncle Len? You don't, do you?

(*Very quietly.*) Every night in her bedroom she hears the scratching, and she thinks it's Dad – that he's in his coffin, clawing at the lid to get out. She starts fucking screaming, going *mental*. I tell her it was just the mice scratching in the walls, try to reassure her, but then she starts saying that it's *him* in the walls. Him. My dad. Stuck there, not able to get out. Alive. Every night.

Pause.

She shouldn't say that sort of shit to me.

LEN. No, she shouldn't.

JEN. It wasn't just her that loved him.

LEN. Yeah, I know.

JEN. We started hearing them the week after he died. My dad dead, and the house suddenly teeming with *life*.

(*Very difficult to say.*) It was really twisting the fucking knife, to be honest.

Long pause. LEN takes the final mouse out of the bag. He holds it above the bucket of water. There's a long pause.

LEN *looks at* JEN *and smiles. He's made a decision.*

LEN (*to the mouse*). You know what I'm going to do to *you*, you cunt? Go on, guess, you little prick. It's something a little bit special.

Long pause.

(*Quietly.*) I'm going to drive you to the fucking country, right, and then I'm going to set you free.

(*Thinks.*) Doubtless you'll get eaten by an owl in like five minutes – it's that kind of owl-eat-mouse world, I'm afraid.

(*Earnestly.*) But, if you *do* survive, you fuck, then one day, when you've got your thousands of rodent grandchildren sitting at your feet wondering why all old folk stink of Ralgex and piss, think of this moment, this defining moment in your little mouse's life.

(*Moves the box closer to his face.*) You know what, mate? Nobody's shown fuck-all mercy to me or her or her mum in this brutal fucking abattoir of a world, have they? Not God, not you, not anybody. But I will to you, mate. Bit of compassion. Fuck knows why. Bit of mercy. That's all.

JEN. Uncle Len?

LEN. Yeah I know – I'm chatting to a mouse.

Long pause.

Come on, Jen – let's fuck off.

(*Smiles.*) You tip out the bucket in the sink, I'll chuck these cunts out. Get your wellies on.

Pause.

JEN. Uncle Len – if we let it go – won't it just come back, like you said?

LEN. Let it. Let it bring all its fucking mates, and all. I fucking dare them. Bring it on. What's going to happen then?

(*Shrugs.*) We'll just have to sit here, the two of us, drowning the wretched cunts. Come on, mate, let's fucking do it – every time you're back from uni.

Pause.

We could make it a thing. You and me.

JEN. I'd like that.

Pause.

I'd like that a lot, Uncle Len.

(*Thinks.*) Every month. I'll come back every month.

LEN. Nice one.

(*Pointing to the can.*) Let me finish this fucker first. I drive like a cunt when I'm sober.

They both leave.

To black.

2. Neither Use Nor Ornament

The same, a month later.

Two chairs and a table.

JEN *enters carrying the bucket. It's the same bucket as the scene before.*

We should assume it's full of mice again.

LEN *follows behind with some newspapers and a broom. He's wearing gloves.*

He puts the newspapers on the table, and the broom against the wall. He finds two very large tubes of superglue, and studies them intently.

LEN. Literally can't believe the state of that room, mate.

JEN. I know.

LEN. *Covered* with body parts like a bomb'd gone off. Fucking war zone, mate.

(*Studies the inside of the bucket.*) I found one piece of head under the sofa and the other half the *complete* other side of the room under the curtains.

(*Checks his shoe.*) Even had some little bits of claw or something stuck to the sole of my shoe where I'd been walking in it.

Beat.

Massacre, mate. Mental.

JEN (*quietly*). I told you it was fucked up.

LEN. Ah, perk the fuck up, mate. We're the fucking Two Musketeers, you and me. We'll sort it, right?

JEN. I don't even know why we're – we're never going to be able to *glue* them back together, are we?

LEN. *Mate.* I'm like fucking Michelangelo with this shit.

(*Holds up the glue.*) Superglue *virtuoso*, right? Good as new.

LEN *lays out the newspaper on the table.*

JEN. That's literally impossible.

LEN. Only one way to find out.

(*Grimly.*) Come on then – tip it out.

JEN *sits down. Poised to pour out the contents of the bucket.*

A moment of tension. What's going to come out of the bucket? Mangled mice?

Nope. She carefully pours out lots of pieces of broken pottery.

I can't believe your mum did that, to be honest.

JEN. I know, right?

LEN. Seriously – I know she's like seriously mad and grieving and that – but as far as I can see clinical depression's completely indistinguishable from being a massive selfish bell end.

JEN. Len.

LEN. What the fuck was she doing trashing your dad's room anyway? Pulling down bookshelves like that – like she's turned into the Laura Ashley version of the Incredible Hulk or something.

JEN. She just isn't herself. Any more.

LEN. Telling me.

JEN. She was trying to find some of Dad's legal stuff. It's all a massive mess, apparently –

LEN (*with considerable understatement*). It is all a massive mess, mate, yes.

Pause.

(*Trying to perk her up.*) Come on, Jen. We *can't* just fuck it off. These cunts were in your dad's study for like thirty years and that – Virgin Mary like this – (*Hands out, palm facing out.*) and Chinese Lucky Cat? The one with the constantly wanking arm? (*Mimes this.*)

JEN. I always thought *waving*, but yeah.

LEN. His good-luck charms.

He sits down next to her.

Pause.

JEN. Didn't *work*, did they?

LEN. What?

JEN. 'Good luck.'

LEN (*trying to enthuse* JEN). Come on, you glum old bastard. We can do this. Me and you.

JEN (*uncertain*). Go on then.

LEN. Booyaka.

Pause. He looks at the broken pottery and smiles.

(*Faux-apprehensive.*) Mate. I've just had a *terrible* thought. Maybe we *should* just fuck this off, and all.

JEN. You've just spent the past half hour trying to persuade me.

LEN (*obviously put on*). Maybe we're... meddling with forces beyond our comprehension.

JEN (*realising she's being wound up, but not quite knowing how*). What?

LEN. Well, use your fucking swede, Jen – if we end up, you know, doing it all wrong and giving the Holy Mother of God a *cat's head* – let alone a wanking arm, Jen – we run the very real risk of getting fucked on by thunderbolts and plagues of frogs and that. Divine retribution, mate. Vengeance. Old school.

JEN (*with a smile*). I think I'll take my chances with that, Len.

LEN. On your head be it, mate.

JEN *smiles. Pause.*

JEN. Okay, I think I've worked out what's what –

(*Starting to sort stuff out.*) All the bits of blue are from Mary's cloak, and all the red and green are Wankycat's ears

and shirt. If we start sorting the colours and go from there...
Do you want to sort, and I'll glue?

LEN. Fuck off.

(*Thinks*.) You're not gluing, no way.

JEN. I'm gluing. You sort.

Beat.

It's my *plan*.

LEN. Fuck you. I'm the *king* of gluing.

(*Holding up the glue*.) And anyway, Jen, this is some serious
fucking shit.

JEN. I think I'll be alright, okay?

LEN. I'm not being funny or anything, but I just don't think you
can handle fucking *gnarly* glue like this. I'm your uncle,
right, and I'm supposed to look after you.

JEN. Fuck you, Len.

(*Quietly*.) I'm gluing.

*Angry pause from JEN. LEN tries to fill the dead space with
words.*

LEN. Seriously, mate – on my mate Shaun's stag some fucker
glued his hand to his, you know – (*Points at his groin*.) dick
while he was passed out at a Travelodge.

(*Points to himself*.) Absolutely *nothing* to do with it, you
understand.

*He looks to JEN for a reaction. She doesn't look at him. He
carries on.*

The doctors were going to yank it off, but they couldn't
because this shit's so massively potent. The fucking screams
off him – (*Screams in agony as a demonstration*.)

He looks again. No reaction.

And he was in tears and that, screaming –

(*Very melodramatic*.) '*Why?*'

Like in some shit film, but then they told him that in a few
days the top layer of skin would be sloughed off naturally
and it'd just work itself apart, like –

He looks again. JEN *starts sorting the pieces into two piles.*

So he spent three days off work, perpetually holding his –
dick – right. His girlfriend was like –

(*Domineering voice.*) '*Three days constantly touching
yourself? A dream come true, I'd have thought, you mucky
bastard –* '

(*Coming to the punchline.*) And he was like –

(*With the suffering voice of Philoctetes.*) '*No, love, the thing
about self-abuse is that it's got to be optional.*' Fucking
legend.

He looks at JEN, *expecting her to find the story funny. She
doesn't.*

Tough crowd. At The Lion they always go mental for that
story. Fat Rob actually shat himself once, laughing at that
story.

JEN. Sorry, Len – I just – it's just you've told me that joke
about a million times.

LEN. Bollocks, have I?

JEN. Every time you're drunk. And Mum told me you made it
up anyway.

LEN. Go on then, mate, go ahead and take a massive
disapproving slash all over my fucking bonfire, then, if it
makes you feel better. Seriously, it's like bantering with
Queen fucking Victoria.

JEN. It's not *true*.

LEN. 'We are not amused' – fuck's sake.

JEN. Whatever, Len.

LEN (*looks around the table, finds a piece*). Now, I reckon this
has pretty much got to be one of the Virgin Mary's tits. For a
two-thousand-year-old she's still fucking perky.

JEN (*mock-offended*). Len. What about thunderbolts?

LEN. You're fucking impossible, mate.

A rather childish silence. They continue with their work.

Mice still gone?

JEN. Mum says so.

LEN (*trying to raise morale again*). Greatest team in the history of the universe, mate, doing that. You and me.

JEN (*not convinced*). Yeah. Batman and Robin, right?

LEN. Right.

Pause.

Couple of cans?

JEN (*with a sigh*). Go on then.

He pulls some cans from his pocket, as before. He opens his.

LEN. Cheers.

She opens hers.

JEN. Cheers.

LEN. Used to sit here with your dad, like this, sometimes. Escape from your mum.

Pause.

Miss it.

There's a long pause. They sip from their cans and stare at the broken pottery. Suddenly everything seems hopeless.

JEN *closes her eyes. She's missing her father very much.*

You holding up?

She nods.

JEN. You?

He nods.

(*Quietly.*) Sometimes it's pretty shit, actually.

LEN. Yeah.

Long pause.

Mate, he was the fucking greatest guy, your dad.

JEN. Yeah.

LEN. People always say that when people [die] – (*Enthusiastically.*) but your dad, right, he was *literally* the greatest fucking guy.

JEN (*tenderly*). Yeah.

Long pause.

Sometimes, when I can't sleep, I play recordings of his radio show for hours, just to hear his voice.

Pause.

Sometimes I can't bear to.

LEN. Yeah.

(*Fills up the awkwardness.*) Your dad, mate – national fucking treasure. Fucking *lad*.

(*Thinks.*) You know what, mate? In terms of a national-treasure fantasy league I reckon the list goes: One – the Queen, two – Winston Churchill, three – your dad, and then four – like Shakespeare or Terry Wogan or some shit like that –

(*Thinks.*) Fuck that, he actually pisses on Winston Churchill, and all – who as far as I know never came in the top three of *Strictly Come Dancing or* got to the top of Everest wearing an abominable snowman costume for *Children in Need* – the fat slobbering wanker –

(*Counts off on fingers.*) So it goes the Queen, and then your dad, and then the rest can stroll the fuck on.

JEN. I know.

LEN. He just had this incredible… *bonhomie* about him – this – *élan* –

(*Thinks*.) Twenty-three front covers of *TV Times*, a
knighthood, and a canteen in the BBC named after him.
That's a fucking legacy, mate. That's a fucking life.

JEN. Yeah.

LEN. He made people feel so –

(*Thinks*.) It was like everybody actually *loved* him.
Everywhere he went people just – hugging him, having their
picture taken – even Nelson Mandela was all giggly like a
schoolgirl when he interviewed him –

JEN (*quietly*). Until last year.

LEN. Fuckers.

JEN. It all just –

LEN. People are fickle fucking cunts. I can't believe how quick
they were to –

JEN. I know.

LEN. Build him up, and then rip him down. Like a pack of
fucking wolves.

JEN. Yeah.

LEN. Of all people in the world, he just didn't deserve that shit.
He was just so –

(*Smiles*.) You know the fuck even bought my house for me?

JEN. No.

LEN. Just wanted to see me clear, the fucking lovely bastard.
Didn't tell your mum, didn't tell anybody. Used to lend me
money when I needed it, which was always, and told me to
repay it when I could, which was never.

(*Smiles*.) Solid fucking gold.

JEN. He was – (*Can't finish this*.) He was just the greatest.

LEN. Yeah, he was.

*They go back to fixing the china. The rhythm of the work
gives them purpose.*

JEN looks at the broken statues. She picks up a piece of Mary's face.

She holds the broken pottery up to her own face.

JEN. You know he used to pray, Uncle Len? After he was arrested – he started to pray – to Mary here. Every day. Never had before. I'd see him on his knees by his bed, for hours. It was actually really heartbreaking to see.

(*Shakes head.*) But Mary, Mary, Quite Contrary here, what did you do? All those prayers. Did you lift a finger to help?

(*Makes an ironically pious face.*) 'Fuck it,' you thought, with your smug fucking smirk all over your face, and left an innocent man to be torn to fucking pieces.

Beat.

Cheers, babe.

She tosses the piece back down.

LEN. That's it, mate. You fucking insult that shard of pottery. Show it who's boss, mate.

JEN. Fuck off.

Pause.

A long pause. They concentrate on mending the pottery. As ever, LEN *needs to fill the conversational void with cheerfulness.*

LEN. Fuck me, this cider *works* so early in the morning.

JEN. I know. My gluing's already very slightly wonky.

LEN. You know what, Jen? From now on I'm getting up before eleven every fucking day. You get trashed on *nothing*. It's fucking awesome. By midday I'll be in fucking Narnia, snogging fauns and shit.

JEN (*deadpan*). Pleased to be part of the change, Len.

The work gives them a feeling of peace.

LEN *is having some success with Wankycat.*

LEN. Look at this, mate. I've got the whole of the fucking head and shoulders back on.

JEN. Let me see.

LEN. No, don't touch it. It's not dry yet.

LEN *has to hold it precariously to stop it falling to pieces.*

JEN (*thinks*). We should get some masking tape or something, help it stick together until it dries.

LEN. Good thinking, Batman. There's some in that drawer over there.

JEN *goes off to find it.*

Me and your dad used to do Airfix kits when we were kids, you know.

JEN. Really?

LEN. I never had the patience. Mine always looked like the Lockerbie-bomb wreckage. Your dad's were always immaculate.

(*Smiles.*) Fucking clever bastard that he was.

Pause.

Fucking think of it often, me and him when we were smaller.

JEN. Yeah.

LEN. Miss that, you know.

JEN. Yeah.

JEN *finds the masking tape.*

Got it.

LEN. Nice one.

They go back to their work.

Another pause.

How's the boyfriend, mate? Taking care of you?

JEN. We're not – any more.

LEN. Oh.

JEN. Turned out he was a prick.

LEN. Almost invariably happens, I'm afraid, with boyfriends. What happened?

JEN. Nothing. When Dad died he just – he just withdrew. He just – (*Mimes holding up hands in surrender.*)

LEN. It's difficult to know how to be around someone, when somebody they love's [died].

JEN. Then one day he asks me how long after my dad's death it would be before I'd 'feel able' to send him a crotch shot again.

LEN *involuntarily drops his porcelain.*

LEN. *Jen* –

(*Looks shocked.*) No way?

JEN. Way.

LEN. I literally can't believe it, Jen.

(*With an ill-suited paternal tone.*) I'm really not happy about you getting yourself caught up in that sort of nonsense, mate.

JEN (*'What the fuck has it got to do with you?'*). You're really not happy about it? Okay then.

(*Reassuring.*) Len. It's alright. I find random porn photos on the internet and send them instead. It's never actually my – bits.

LEN (*relieved*). Oh, good girl. Dad's brains, that.

JEN (*trying to start up repartee to rescue the situation*). Although it's actually a funny story, Len – you know – the photos are from different women each time – so if he'd ever done a slide-show of them on his computer he'd totally have thought that I've got some kind of weird shape-shifting genitalia, like – (*Mimes snapping jaws like a crocodile.*) I'm coming to get you, the shape-shifting vagina! Ahhh!

LEN. Jen. That's revolting. Come on.

JEN. What? It's just a – like – joke, Len.

LEN. I just don't want to hear bawdy fucking stories about my niece's vagulica, you know?

(*Mildly pleading tone.*) I used to fucking bath you when you were a baby – fuck's sake, Jen.

JEN. You've gone all red, Uncle Len.

LEN. I've not.

JEN. You have.

LEN (*frustrated and flustered*). I just don't like to hear sketchy talk like that, that's all.

JEN. Right. And you're not a massive fucking hypocrite or anything, then.

LEN. No, mate, I'm not actually.

JEN. Right then. Your genitalia story, great – mine, *verboten*. Brilliant.

Awkward silence. They go back to their work.

LEN. I'm fucking smashing this now, Jen. Fucking *catty* this is now.

JEN. Good.

Pause.

LEN. I'm sorry, Jen, alright? For being a wanker.

JEN. You're not a wanker.

LEN. I am, mate. It's a truth universally acknowledged.

Pause.

But I'm listening, alright? I'm interested in your shit. Well, not your *shit* in a German way, you know – (*German porn-film voice.*) '*Ja ja, Jennifer, scheisse in meine face, das ist sehr gut*' – (*Normal voice.*) but your *shit*. You know.

JEN (*halfway between irony and sincerity*). Thanks.

LEN (*sincerity is awkward*). And I'm here. You know. For you. Whatever that means. Right fucking here.

Pause. She thinks about it.

JEN (*awkward*). Can I tell you something else, Uncle Len?

LEN. Of course, mate. As long as it's not another off-colour joke about your vagulica, mate, crack the fuck on.

JEN. Len.

LEN. Sorry. I'm all fucking ears.

JEN. It's just that I don't have a whole bunch of people I can talk to about it.

LEN (*quietly*). No. Nor me.

JEN (*deep breath*). At uni, just after Dad [died], this guy came up to me, wasted, at some party, and he said to me:

(*Posh voice.*) 'Oh, yah, Jen, right? Is it actually true that your pervy fucking dad used to massively fuck you too and stuff, when you were growing up? It's *totally* what everybody's saying.'

LEN (*really upset*). Jen –

JEN. And then he was like – 'You know what, Jen? Play your cards right, I can do a *fucking* good impression of his voice if you want to come back to mine and relive your childhood.'

Pause.

And I just ran away. All the way home. Back here.

LEN (*angrily protective*). If you show me who that cunt was, Jen, I'll fucking rip his head off, mate. I'll fucking gut the prick.

JEN. Len.

LEN. Seriously, mate – that's fucking outrageously awful.

JEN. Len. It happens.

Pause.

The weird thing is that I actually think he was actually trying to pull me.

LEN. I'll fucking cut his cock off, the little cunt.

JEN. Yeah. So I'm thinking about leaving uni. I mean, I pretty much have to.

LEN (*emphatically*). You can't, mate. You can't let one wanker fuck up everything like that.

JEN. I know that in principle, Len – but, you know? I don't know if I can hack it any more because – everybody knows. About Dad. Everybody's always staring at me, all the fucking time. Making jokes, whispering behind their hands.

LEN. Mate. You've got to style it the fuck out. For your dad. It's what he would have wanted.

JEN (*that wasn't the comfort she wanted*). Yeah. Thanks.

LEN. It's just one guy, one time.

JEN. It's not, Len.

Pause.

Because what really gets me isn't the *cruel* wankers twisting the knife. It's the *kind* people trying to be *nice*.

(*Another posh voice.*) '*Totes sorry about your dead dad, babes.*' Everybody's so fucking *inane* about it. They talk to me like I'm retarded or something, just because my dad's dead – I mean, fuck's sake, it's my heart it tore out, not my fucking brain, you fucking cunts.

She delivers this with impassioned violence. LEN doesn't know how to reply.

LEN. Yeah. It's shit, isn't it?

Pause.

JEN. Sorry.

LEN. Mate.

Pause.

JEN. What about you? You working at the moment?

LEN. Sabbatical.

JEN. How long?

LEN. Since your dad [died]. The fucks on the site just won't let it go either. Thing is with jokes, right – they're all fucking funny when it's not the lurid details of your dead brother's historical sex-offences trial they're taking the piss out of.

Pause.

JEN (*awkward*). So – are you – are you okay for money, Len? If you're not working and things.

LEN. Fuck yes. Fucking sorted.

JEN. You sure?

LEN. I'm a fucking wily bastard, Jen. I've got a whole fucking string of schemes and dodges sorted.

JEN. What like?

LEN (*quietly*). I'll just be fine, okay?

JEN. Len?

LEN (*changing the subject*). Is that a bit of the Virgin Mary's girdle or whatever, or is it the bell off Wankycat's neck?

JEN (*disappointed that he doesn't want to talk about it*). That's a piece of bell, I reckon. Different colour gold to the other bits.

She fumbles the bit she's trying to fix. It drops on the floor.

Bollocks.

LEN *looks under the table.*

LEN. Don't worry, mate. I can see it.

JEN. Where?

LEN. Just there.

JEN. I'll get it.

LEN. You're alright. Least I can fucking do.

He gets it.

JEN. Thanks, Len.

LEN. No worries. What would your mum say?

(*Strong Yorkshire accent.*) '*You're neither use nor ornament, Jen.*'

JEN. Good old Mum – the sort of total annihilation of personality you can only get from a proper Yorkshire put-down.

LEN. You're lucky. I never even merited an insult. Proper beneath contempt.

JEN. I *dream* of being beneath contempt, Len.

Pause.

LEN. Fuck, I can't see any more of this ear. Have you got a bit of ear?

Pause.

JEN. You know what, Len? Last term I watched a friend of mine in a play – *Oedipus Rex.*

LEN (*with utter lack of sincerity*). 'Mazin'.

JEN *looks at him for a second.*

JEN. The last line was – 'count no man happy until he's dead.'

LEN. Oh yeah?

JEN. I've been thinking about that a lot since Dad [died]. The last year of Dad's life was a fucking nightmare. But you know what? That was one year in fifty. The rest of his life was pretty much awesome for him, I reckon. And I keep trying to reassure myself – one year in fifty – that still makes his life ninety-eight-per-cent happy, right? That's pretty good statistics, right?

Pause.

But it doesn't work like that, does it?

LEN. No, it doesn't.

Long pause. LEN *is thinking about something.*

Jen.

JEN. What?

LEN (*earnestly*). Can I tell you some shit, and all?

JEN. What, Len?

LEN. It's fucking dark shit.

JEN (*with a hint of a smile*). I'm the queen of dark shit, Len. Not in a German way, you know?

LEN. Sorry – it's just I'm not good at – you know.

Painful pause.

He called me. Your dad. The night he –

JEN (*quietly*). The night he died?

LEN. Eleven in the evening – and I didn't see the call.

(*Shrugs sadly.*) I was out getting fucked.

Pause.

Rips the fucking heart out of me that I didn't take that call, Jen.

(*Quietly.*) Tears me to fucking bits.

JEN. Eleven o'clock?

(*Trying to reassure him.*) He'd almost certainly taken the pills by then, Len. There was nothing you could have done –

LEN. Yeah, well.

(*Looks down at the floor.*) The whole thing was so fucking *meticulous*, wasn't it? Books a suite at Claridge's, has dinner, orders some fine brandy, smashes his pills, falls asleep –

Pause.

– fucking *considerate* way out if you think about it.

JEN (*with an edge of rawness*). *Considerate* isn't really the word I'd – use.

LEN. If he'd done it here, in this house – that'd have been much worse, wouldn't it?

JEN. It couldn't possibly have been *worse*.

LEN. You finding him – your mum? Here? Dead?

Pause.

But then he calls me at eleven – just about the same time as he takes the pills, I reckon. Didn't phone anyone else.

(*Painfully.*) And I was shitted in the pub.

(*Very slowly.*) Wanted to talk. And I let him down. Last thing that happened to him, the last thing he was aware of in this life before he killed himself – was me letting him down.

JEN *has no answer to this.*

JEN. Len.

LEN. Mate, there's pretty much fuck-all you can say at this juncture –

JEN. I know.

Pause.

(*Trying to lighten the mood.*) You know that room cost eighteen hundred pounds? Eighteen hundred. For a hotel room. For one night.

(*With an attempt to cheer him up.*) I suppose You Only Die Once, right?

LEN. Yeah.

JEN. YODO.

LEN (*with a smile*). Fuck off, mate.

Pause.

JEN *looks down at the fragments.*

JEN. Mary and Wankycat here – neither use nor ornament, are they? And look at us, Len. No better.

LEN (*forces himself to lighten the mood*). Speak for yourself, love. I've always considered myself one of the world's hottest middle-aged scumbags, to be honest. I've always thought I could be a proper centrefold skank, all posing like this – (*Mimes erotic pose.*) *Un can de cidre* strategically protecting my modesty.

(*Pointing at his crotch.*) '*Earn it.*'

She looks at him with a smile.

JEN. Len – people cross the road to avoid you with alarm in their faces.

LEN. That's because they can't trust themselves not to leap bodily upon me.

JEN (*kindly*). Whatever.

LEN (*looking down at the smashed ruins in front of him*). Shall we fuck this off, Jen?

JEN (*resolute*). No. Let's get it done, Len. Even if we have to sit here all night, and no matter how shit they look at the end, let's put all this shit back together.

LEN. Why?

JEN. Because we're not going to let this beat us, Len.

LEN. It doesn't mean anything, Jen, this – it's just broken china.

JEN. I know, Len. I know.

Sudden fade to black.

3. Dies Iræ

The stage is empty for a while.

JEN (*off; angry, hurt*). How could *anyone* do that, Len? I –

It's just so unbelievably fucking – *cruel*.

LEN (*off*). Mate.

JEN comes in, very upset.

LEN follows several steps behind.

JEN. If Mum finds out, it's going to kill her. Simple as.

Pause.

What the fuck are we going to do, Len?

(*Angry, frustrated.*) Fuck it all.

Perhaps she kicks something out of rage.

She sits on the floor in the corner of the room. Head in her hands.

LEN pulls a can out of his pocket.

LEN (*kindly*). Get that down you, mate.

He holds it out in her direction. She doesn't take it. He puts it down in front of her.

He sits next to her.

Silence.

It's just twats, Jen.

JEN. They trampled every single fucking flower on his grave, Len. Every single fucking one.

LEN. It's just pissed kids. Don't let it get to you.

JEN. Get to me? Fuck's sake – they pulled up his cross, and they snapped it. Pissed kids.

LEN (*quietly*). I saw, Jen.

(*Trying to mitigate.*) It's only the *temporary* cross, mate.

JEN (*almost laughing with frustration and incomprehension*). And the twat who sprayed '*Paedo*' on his fucking memorial bench, Len? Nobody's ever even *accused* him of that, for fuck's sake.

LEN (*with a shrug*). Least they spelt it right.

JEN. If I ever find out who did it, I'm going to rip their fucking heads off.

LEN. And what the fuck's that going to solve?

JEN. It's Dad's fucking [grave]…

LEN. I know, Jen.

A long silence. At the end punctuated by LEN *opening his can.*

Come on, mate.

JEN. No.

Long pause.

I just *can't*.

Pause.

Anything.

Pause.

He left me on my fucking own. To deal with all this shit.

LEN. You're not on your own, mate. Look. (*Points to his own face.*)

JEN. I fucking need him, Len.

LEN. I know, mate. Me too.

Pause.

JEN (*change of tone – quieter*). Thanks for coming, Len. When I called you.

LEN. Course I'd come, you daft bastard. I keep my phone on these days, you know?

JEN. I sometimes go early in the morning –

LEN. Me too.

JEN *cracks open her can*.

JEN (*looking at her watch*). Nine a.m. A new record.

LEN. Speak for yourself, love.

Pause.

You know what we need to do, Jen?

JEN. Die?

LEN *looks hard at* JEN.

LEN. I don't want you ever saying that again, right?

JEN *looks down*.

We're going to get all the cleaning things out, and we're going to sort out the bench with another coat of wood stain, then we're going to the garden centre to buy new fucking pansies and hyacinths and all that gay shit, and then we're going to go to Lake's when he opens and buy another cross off of him. In a couple of hours it'll be good as new, I swear it.

(*Looks seriously at* JEN.) And we're not going to tell your mum or anybody else about it, right?

JEN. We're not going to be able to *fix* it, Len.

LEN. Bet your fucking life we are.

JEN. They'll just do it again. The cunts.

LEN. Then we'll fix it again. And again. And again if we have to.

JEN. It's pointless.

LEN. It's absolutely not pointless, is it, Jen?

(*With a smile*.) Come on, get your drink on, and let's fuck off.

He looks at her expectantly.

JEN. Fuck it, Len. Just fuck it.

> LEN *gets up anyway, and collects the bucket, and some sponges, and some cleaning fluid.*

LEN. We'll want you, and you, and this bugger too.

> (*To* JEN.) There's a tap at the churchyard, right?

> JEN *nods, almost imperceptibly.*

> *He finds a tin of wood stain and a paintbrush.*

We'll need this bugger. And this and all.

> *He puts these in the bucket too.*

Right, you coming?

> JEN *thinks.*

JEN. No, Len. I can't.

LEN. I need your help, Jen.

JEN. I'm not going to be much – good to you.

LEN. I literally don't think I can do this on my own.

> *He waits for her to join him.*

JEN. I can't do it, Len. I'm sorry.

LEN (*kindly, disappointed*). It's all right. I understand. You've got your own shit to deal with.

> *He leaves.*

> JEN *sits by herself for a few moments. Head in her hands, then looking up to the ceiling.*

> *Finally she looks over to the door.*

> *Suddenly to black.*

4. Bin Bags

The same, a month later.

Two chairs. The chairs are surrounded by piles of very full black bin bags.

LEN *sits on a chair, his head in his hands.*

JEN *is standing staring at him. She's nervous and on edge, but trying to hide it with banter.*

JEN. Len? *Mate?*

LEN. It's fucking ghoulish, mate, this.

    JEN *gestures towards the bin bags.* LEN *doesn't reply.*

JEN (*saying this to convince herself as much as him*). Come on, Uncle Len – don't be such a massive *hom*.

    Beat.

    Man the F – U.

    Pause.

    (*Bravado instead of courage.*) Have you got any cans, mate? Like we normally do? Make it a *thing*?

LEN. I'm not a fucking human vending machine, Jen. No.

    He takes two cans from his pockets.

    Here.

JEN. Thanks.

LEN. Too early for me, sweetheart.

    He cracks open the can.

    JEN *sits next to him.*

JEN. She was going to take it to the tip.

LEN (*points to the bags*). It's his *life*.

JEN. I know. At the very least it should go to Oxfam so that *somebody* benefits.

LEN. I can actually picture it – a bunch of African child soldiers, holding AKs vastly too big for 'em, kitted out in oversized Harris tweed and Pringle jumpers like miniature Bertie fucking Woosters.

(*Wooster voice.*) '*Is it grouse we're shooting today, what what, or Tutsis?*'

JEN. Christ's sake, Len. That's dark.

(*Looks at him seriously.*) They sell it.

LEN. I know. I'm not a *spastic*. I was – fuck it.

Long pause.

JEN (*with difficulty*). I just want to get to – well – a position where I can go from being like *this* to just being really, really fucking sad, okay?

LEN *looks at her with compassion.*

And I just think doing this will *help*.

(*Trying to phrase it correctly.*) It's not that I want to *move on*, Len, I just want to be able to *keep going*.

(*With a smile.*) I know it's just *stuff* – but I – it's his life.

Long pause. Very miserable.

LEN (*singing, quietly*). '*Ain't no party like a Jen and Len party, cus a Jen and Len party it don't stop.*'

LEN *clinks his can against* JEN's. JEN *reluctantly gives him a smile. He picks up a hammer from the table.*

'*Alright stop: Hammertime!*'

JEN *doesn't react.*

Yeah, well. That's a different fucking song, isn't it?

JEN. Yeah.

LEN. Different decade and everything. Never knew what the fuck *Hammertime* was supposed to be anyway. The only thing I've ever been able to visualise was that chap off the news who killed his two elderly parents with a claw hammer.

JEN. Didn't hear about that.

LEN. Yeah. Couple of years back. Unmarried man in his fifties, parents in their eighties. All a bit weird and incesty and stuff. Anyway, do you reckon he went up to them and went, '*Alright stop, Hammertime?*' and then mashed up their heads?

(*Mimes murder in light-hearted nineties hip-hop manner.*) I can actually picture it – he's standing over their mangled bodies with triumph and horror etched onto his face, and he points to his father-abused genitalia and he's all like – (*Sings.*) '*You can't touch this.*'

(*Philosophically.*) Fucking chilling, Hammertime.

JEN. I don't think I've ever actually heard the song.

LEN. No way?

JEN. No.

LEN. Well then, that must have meant practically nothing at all to you, then.

JEN. Not really.

LEN. Yeah well. Pretty fucking seminal song for me.

Pause.

Sometimes, mate, the gap between the generations yawns as wide as a fucking chasm, doesn't it? It's like we're from different planets or something.

JEN. I've always kinda assumed you were from a different planet, Len, yes.

LEN. Yeah.

Pause.

Why's that fucking bitch so fucking keen to chuck out all his stuff anyway…? Fucking evil fucking banshee witch fishwife cunt that she is.

JEN. Len – come on, mate.

LEN. Sorry. I don't know why she's in such a fucking rush to obliterate every fucking trace of him.

JEN. Granny's moving into his old study. Need the space.

LEN (*trying to cheer her up*). Fuck. Medusa and the fucking Minotaur in one house? It's getting fucking *Old School* in here.

JEN. Len. Turns out Dad had pretty overwhelming debts. Legal fees. Death duties. Granny's selling her house so we can keep ours.

LEN. Fuck.

JEN. And she says Granny being here will help her with her depression and stuff.

LEN. Fuck off – that's like getting Nosferatu in to… nurse a ward of… haemophiliacs.

JEN. I was away at uni. There's things of his I'd like to keep. I wasn't even asked. Mementos.

LEN. Bitch.

JEN. And then, to make the whole thing a million times worse, she fucking *forbade* me from looking through the stuff. Like she was the only one that mattered.

LEN. See? Bitch.

JEN (*brightening a touch*). But to be honest, Len, you could use some new clothes.

LEN. I'm not wearing his stuff. Fuck's sake.

JEN. Everything you've got on is his cast-off clothes. Always has been.

LEN. He was always very good at looking after me, the twat.

Pause.

JEN (*with resolution*). Right – you go through the clothes, I'll do the books. Three piles – keepers, Oxfam, bin.

LEN. Seriously, Jen, I still reckon this is fucking bad juju, alright?

JEN. Please, Len. Just go with me on this.

LEN. Seriously, Jen. It's his private shit.

JEN. It's *fine*.

LEN. Everybody's got secrets and shit, Jen. Stuff you'd not want people delving into and that.

JEN. I don't.

LEN (*with a sudden flash of trapped frustration*). You send photos of other people's wookies to your boyfriend so he can toss off over them, Jen.

Beat.

And then you lie about those wookies' provenance, for fuck's sake.

LEN *instantly regrets the outburst.*

Sorry.

JEN. That's alright.

Beat.

Wookies?

LEN. You know – like Wookey Hole Caves.

JEN (*winces*). Oh.

LEN. But with the added, you know, resonance of Chewbacca – that sort of Wookiee – (*Does an impression of Chewbacca noise.*) *Star Wars*?

JEN. Right.

LEN. But it doesn't really work these days, you know – bloody great hairy buggers, aren't they, Wookiees?

JEN. Yeah.

LEN. And girls these days – I mean more than likely *you're* shaved – (*This is now very awkward.*) or waxed. Down there. Sorry.

JEN (*wishes this would all stop*). O – *kay*.

LEN (*slightly desperate*). And I always think, Jen, if you were to shave Chewbacca, what would you be left with? Just a really big mentally handicapped guy.

JEN. Len.

LEN. And I actually feel broadly the same about shaved vagulicas, mate.

Beat.

Sorry.

JEN. Len. For fuck's sake.

LEN (*changing tone*). Let's leave it at that, right?

JEN (*disbelieving*). Let's.

Pause.

LEN. Come on then. Let's fucking crack on.

They pull a bag out each and untie them.

(*Takes out a sweater.*) What's this bugger? I don't ever remember him wearing this. Too small for me.

(*Thinks.*) Oxfam.

JEN*'s bag is full of books and paper.*

JEN (*taking out some books*). Okay. Dictionary, book about the English Garden Through the Ages, cricket. Oxfam.

LEN (*another sweater*). This one's got a hole in the elbow.

(*Thinks.*) Bin.

(*Another one.*) Toxic Christmas jumper. Bin.

JEN (*another book*). Eighties political cartoons. Oxfam.

LEN (*takes out another jumper*). This is the bollocks. Keep.

(*To* JEN, *happily*.) Hey, this is easier than I thought, Jen.

So, seeing anyone at the moment?

JEN. No.

(*With an impish smile.*) Come here often?

LEN. Fuck off. Avuncular concern, you know?

JEN. Yeah.

LEN. How's uni?

JEN. Fine.

Long pause.

LEN (*struggling to find things to say*). So what music are you listening to these days?

JEN (*shrugs, trying to keep a straight face*). All kinds.

LEN. Great.

JEN. Great.

LEN. Not '*Hammertime*', though, clearly.

JEN. Not so much.

LEN. Fuck it, then.

She takes out a box.

It's fucking weird to think that somebody will have to do this for every single one of us, isn't it?

JEN (*not really listening*). Yeah.

LEN. Every life ends in some pissed-off friend or relative making a series of dreary trips to the tip to chuck out all the precious shit you've so assiduously collected over a lifetime.

JEN (*hasn't heard any of this*). Yeah.

LEN. It doesn't amount to much, does it, a life?

They continue sorting in silence for a while.

JEN (*delight, surprise, nostalgia*). Oh my God. What's this?

She opens it. Pause.

This is all the Christmas cards I ever sent him.

(*Quietly.*) He kept them.

JEN *is very, very touched by this.* LEN *doesn't notice.*

(*Looking through the cards.*) Look at this one. I'd have been six.

(*Very tenderly.*) God, I wrote like I had Parkinson's.

LEN (*taking out another jumper*). This is fucking gash, this one. I wouldn't even give this to the starving Africans. It looks like it's been dipped in a bucket of pig diarrhoea. Bin.

JEN. Len.

(*Looks at the box.*) Yeah, well, this is fucking poignant.

(*Looks up.*) Not the pig-poo jumper –

LEN (*takes out some trousers*). Mint, these. I never understood how his trousers never wore through at the bollocks like mine. I literally must have barbed-wire pubes or something – either that or his were as cashmere.

(*Holds them up to himself.*) What do you reckon, Jen? Can I rock houndstooth slacks?

JEN (*without even looking*). You'll look like a serial killer in them.

(*To the box.*) Keep.

She puts the box in the keep pile.

LEN. You weren't even looking.

JEN. Totally *Crimewatch*.

(*Takes out some books.*) Shit, Len, we can't throw these out, either. Look – *Brothers Karamazov*, Beckett, Tolstoy. Keep.

LEN*'s already bored.*

LEN. Shall we just fuck this off and chuck your gran in the tip instead? Put all this lot back?

JEN. I know.

(*Takes out a folder.*) Christ, look at this?

LEN*'s not looking.*

LEN (*takes out another sweater*). This one? Do you think I'd look more distinguished in diamond-knit?

JEN. Look – it's letters of thanks from all the charities he worked with. Dozens of them.

LEN. Jen?

JEN (*flicking through the pages of the folder*). Cancer, disadvantaged children, half a million pounds for mental health climbing Everest – it's endless. Polar bears. Limbless soldiers. Emotionally scarred donkeys.

(*With a smile.*) Wow.

LEN. Diamond-knit?

JEN. Textbook schizophrenic.

LEN. No offence but fuck off.

(*Actually hurt.*) I'll look like fucking Clooney, alright? Composed. Suave. So unthreatening it's actually kinda threatening.

JEN (*more books*). These can all go. Review copies or something.

(*Takes out* Hamlet. *Wistfully.*) Hamlet – lucky fucker. At least he got to see *his* dad again after he died.

LEN *is trying on the diamond-knit sweater.*

LEN. What do you reckon?

JEN *stares at him.*

So fly you're pondering incest?

JEN (*wistfully*). You actually look a bit like him, you know? In that.

LEN. Yeah – exactly the same features in a different order – his arranged with exquisite care, mine just *tossed* onto my face, like an employee with a grudge at Madame Tussauds.

JEN *laughs.*

The thing is, Jen. I always thought we were somehow *connected* because we were brothers, like we were two peas out the same pod – although admittedly there'd have to have been one really fucked-up misshapen skanky pea and then one really, you know, *gourmet* pea in the same pod, which would have been unlikely, you know? *Botanically* I mean.

(*Suddenly serious*.) You know what, Jen? The fact that me and your dad were close was the only thing in my life I was actually proud of, right? And when all that shit happened to him I thought 'right – fucking go to it, mate – brother the shit out of him'. We used to sit together, right here, and we used to drink cans, just like we are now.

(*Slowly*.) I thought I was winning. But when it came down to it, when it really fucking mattered – I didn't make fuck-all difference, did I?

JEN. Len.

LEN. Didn't even see it coming. Fucking good job there, Len.

(*With a very sad smile*.) And now here I am, twatting about in his clothes like I'm at some ghoulish fancy-dress party.

JEN. Len.

LEN (*ironically*). Good job, mate. Nice one, Len.

JEN. You did all you could.

LEN. Yeah, well.

JEN. Seriously.

LEN. Yeah.

JEN. I sort of *assumed* he would have been too strong, you know, to – to put us through all this shit –

(*Instantly regretful*.) I didn't mean that.

LEN. I know.

JEN. If I saw him right now I don't know whether I'd hug him or smack him one. Both, probably.

LEN. Same.

(*Thinks*.) Although you'd potentially run out of hands, wouldn't you? Hugging and smacking him at the same time. Fucking awkward, that.

JEN. What?

LEN. It'd be fucking easy if you were Ganesh.

JEN. What?

LEN. Indian elephant god.

JEN. Six arms, right?

LEN. Yeah. Fucking handy, that. And if you take into account
the prehensile trunk as well, it gives you a fucking shitload
of extra options.

JEN. *Prehensile*. Good word.

LEN. Pub-quiz word, that.

JEN. Yeah.

LEN. Yeah.

   Pause.

   (*Trying to change the subject.*) You know I got barred from
   The Lion?

JEN. No.

LEN. There was this proper little prick he was always giving
it this about your dad, saying he was getting what's
coming to him – (*Chatting-hand symbol.*) And in the end I
just lost it.

   (*Mimes punching.*) Shanked him.

JEN (*half-disbelief, half-concern*). You didn't *shank* him, Len.
Did you?

LEN. I fucking did. Absolutely *shanked* him one.

JEN. So you *stabbed* him with a knife?

LEN. No, course not.

   (*Twigs.*) Oh right...

   (*Suddenly concerned.*) Fuck.

JEN. What?

LEN. Ah it's probably nothing. It's just – Shaun's kid was getting bullied at school so I gave him some man-to-man advice –

Beat.

I mean he's not actually going to *stab* them, is he? He's seven. Is he?

JEN (*uncertain*). No.

LEN. Course not.

Pause.

(*Back into story.*) Anyway – so I was punching the head off this guy, and Shaun told me not to bother coming in again. My best mate.

JEN. But you've been going there for like twenty-five years, haven't you? Practically every day.

LEN (*with pride*). Every *single* day. Never missed a single one.

(*With forced bonhomie.*) Oh, you know, turned out for the best. Now I have to trek a full five miles to The White Horse in Bagham Bridge. I'm getting fucking outdoorsy, Jen. Jog it sometimes, like fucking Rocky.

(*Mimes running like Rocky, punching in the air.*) Taken ten years off me. Fresh air. It's like I've turned over a new leaf.

Beat.

Miss it, though.

JEN. Yeah.

They go back to their work.

LEN. You know Shaun, don't you? Landlord at The Lion?

JEN. Maybe.

LEN. Fat chap, shaved head, lots of tats. Not like totally fat, you know – *pie-curious*, but not fully out the fat closet.

(*Suddenly serious.*) I was talking to him about your dad.

JEN (*really not interested in Shaun's opinion*). Oh?

LEN. You know – he and the regulars were trying to work out whether he'd, you know, done it and I was saying, you know –

JEN (*very emphatically*). He didn't do it, Len.

LEN. No.

(*Backtracking*.) And that was exactly what I was trying to say to him –

JEN. He *didn't* do it.

LEN. I know, mate, but –

JEN. So then there's no doubting it, or discussing it, is there? Especially not *down the pub*.

LEN. No. I suppose.

JEN (*seriously*). Look, Len. All the women who accused him, Len – and the, you know, men – they're fucking – I mean, some of them probably have shit going on in their lives, mental delusional shit and stuff, which is massively sad – but some of them – I can't help thinking that some of them just want the fucking – to get in the newspapers or something – and that's… fucking *evil* if you ask me.

LEN. Jen.

JEN. Ten people – so everybody automatically goes 'no smoke without fire' – but you can totally find ten mentalists – you know, on pretty much every bus you go on in London –

LEN. Jen. Come on.

JEN. The thought of my dad even *touching* them. It's *ridiculous* – that's not the word – it's totally *impossible*.

Pause.

I *knew* him, Len. I knew him better than anybody.

LEN. I know, mate.

JEN. And even if they actually found him innocent – there've now been so many of these historical sex trials, people just *forget* what the verdict actually was – and even though most of them were innocent – were *found* innocent – there's this horrible *taint* over people for ever, for no reason at all – and so he was fucked either way.

LEN. I know, mate.

JEN. You know what was weird, though?

LEN. What, mate?

JEN. I knew some of them –

LEN. Me too.

JEN. And I – fuck it.

LEN. What?

JEN. I don't know, Len. I – some of them were alright.

LEN. Yeah.

Pause.

JEN. A thirty-year career in radio, Len – and then one day people suddenly start spitting at you in the supermarket.

LEN. Yeah.

JEN. He was my dad, Len. He wasn't like that.

LEN. You know what I think, Jen?

JEN. No, what do you *think*, Len?

LEN. It was all supposed to be twenty-five fucking years ago anyway.

(*Thinks how to phrase it.*) You know when every now and then when they arrest some frail old ninety-year-old pensioner for something they did like seventy years ago in the war? That's not right, Jen, is it?

JEN. No, fuck off, Len.

LEN. No – you know what I mean. The whole thing was half a fucking lifetime ago. It's not the same person you're arresting, is it? I mean – I read somewhere that every seven years every single cell of your body is replaced – so it's literally not even *technically* the same person.

JEN. Len, fuck off – seriously –

LEN. People change, Jen. It was more than half his lifetime
ago. There's got to be some kind of statute of limitations on
– a bit of pity, a bit of mercy –

(Emphatically.) Everybody just needs to let it fucking go, right.

JEN. Len, it doesn't fucking matter how long ago it was, right?
It. Didn't. Fucking. Happen.

LEN. Should I still be punished for shit I did at school, Jen?

JEN. Len, shut the fuck up –

LEN. It's the same thing.

JEN. You're literally a moron.

LEN. No, mate. It's just that I think –

JEN. You don't fucking *think*, though, do you, Len? You never
fucking think. You just sit there, shitfaced, talking crap.

LEN. Come on, mate.

JEN. You're a fucking idiot, Len, alright?

LEN. Mate.

Long pause.

JEN. I didn't mean that, Len.

LEN. Nah, you're right, mate. Fucking moron, me.

JEN. Len.

LEN. Mate, it's water off a retarded duck's back.

JEN. It's just that, with Dad –

LEN. I know, mate.

JEN. I *know* he didn't do it.

LEN. Yeah.

Pause.

JEN. You know *how* I know it didn't happen? Why I'm
absolutely *certain*?

LEN. No?

JEN. Fuck it – I'm not –

LEN. Come on, mate –

JEN. You'll just –

LEN. What?

JEN. Take the piss or try to –

LEN. I won't. Scout's honour.

JEN. Really?

LEN. Really.

JEN. I know for certain he didn't do it –

> (*Very quietly.*) Because it happened to me.

LEN. What?

JEN (*quietly*). Not exactly the same, but –

> *Pause.*

> I was really wasted at a party one time at uni and a guy – some fat fuck of a rugby player called Dom – pushed me against a wall and stuck his hands down my trousers.

LEN. Jen –

JEN. And he was a fucking disgusting, Len – a fucking arrogant, repellent – whispering to me like he was in some porn film, like he thought I actually wanted him to.

LEN. Jen.

JEN. I was too out of it to do anything about it, you see. If my friend hadn't come along and fucking punched him one –

> *Pause.*

> And that guy he was *nothing* like Dad. Nothing at all. Dad was –

LEN. Jen, I –

JEN. Len, that guy who did that to me, Len, he was a revolting fucking beast – and my dad? He was the best human being that I've ever met. So it's literally impossible, isn't it?

(Takes a breath.) So you fucking take it back that you think he did it.

LEN. I don't think he did it.

JEN. No. You don't.

LEN. No.

You're right, mate.

JEN. I'm sorry, I.

LEN. Don't be. I'm sorry.

They go back to their work. LEN *takes out a pair of socks and puts them over his ears.*

(Awkwardly, trying to break the ice again.) Look, Jen, I'm feeling really *ruff* this morning.

(Barks.) Woof!

JEN *turns to look at him. She stares at him critically for a second.*

JEN *(icily)*. Right.

LEN. Woof!

JEN *(rolling her eyes)*. Fuck off.

LEN *(finally, pathetically)*. Woof?

(Disappointed.) Oh, fuck it then. You were much more fun when you were five, Jen. When you were five you'd have been literally pissing yourself with that one.

Long pause. Sorting clothes again.

(Different clothes.) Oxfam, Oxfam, Oxfam.

(Pair of socks.) Soxfam.

JEN *pulls out a red, bound, lined journal book. And another. And another.*

JEN. Oh my God. Here it is.

LEN. What?

JEN. His diary.

LEN. His what?

JEN (*offhand*). His diary. I wonder where Mum found it?

LEN. What?

(*Suddenly very tense*.) When did he start writing a *diary*, Jen?

JEN (*delighted*). The whole of my life. Look – this one's from 1988. 1995. Fifteen minutes every night.

LEN (*in very measured tones*). You want to put that back, Jen.

JEN (*genuinely surprised*). What do you mean?

LEN (*emphatically*). You don't want to go reading it.

JEN. What?

LEN (*with an edge*). Seriously. Put those fuckers back.

JEN (*getting annoyed too*). Shut up, Len.

LEN. Just – please – Jen.

JEN. Why are you being so weird about this?

LEN *thinks for a long time about how to phrase it*.

LEN. I know how much you loved your dad, right?

JEN. What?

LEN. I just don't want you to read stuff in there that would make you – disappointed.

JEN. What are you talking about?

LEN. He settled down a lot when he had you. But before –

JEN. What?

LEN. We used to drink cans, like this. When he was younger he was always boasting about the girls he was with. Even after he was married.

JEN. *Dad?*

LEN. He filled his boots. He was young and famous, and he loved it. He was very, you know, 'treat them mean, keep them keen', and I guess he kind of –

JEN. You're winding me up, right?

LEN. And then, after the whole thing with the trial came up he told me something one afternoon.

JEN. What did he *tell* you, Len?

LEN (*slowly*). He looked at me with tears in his eyes, right – and he told me that he had this hard little ball of dark in his heart, right, and that all the charity stuff and the kindness and the nice-guy routine on the radio – that was just putting layers of good over it, like how those fucking oysters make pearls. But it was still there.

(*Imploringly.*) I don't want you to read anything in there that you wouldn't want to hear.

JEN. That doesn't mean anything.

LEN. It was like a confession. I took it as a confession.

JEN. You're fucking lying.

LEN. Jen. Please. Don't read that fucking diary, alright.

JEN. Shut the fuck up, Uncle Len –

LEN. Jen. Let it go to the tip like your mother wanted.

JEN stares at the diary in her hand.

Suddenly to black.

5. Absolutely Immaculate

LEN *is clearing the shelves of the garage and packing everything in a large removals box.*

He's bored. He clicks the button of an old hi-fi. Loud music. 'U Can't Touch This', by MC Hammer.

He starts packing in time to the music. Eventually he starts really dancing – singing into a shoe brush as a microphone, that sort of thing.

He's really into it. Really enjoying himself.

LEN. Alright stop! Hammertime.

> JEN *comes in, looking tired and dejected. She's carrying a box with bubble wrap spilling out of it.*
>
> *He stops. He gestures for her to dance too. She refuses.*
>
> *He goes over to her, dancing, hoping she'll join in. She rolls her eyes and sits down on one of the chairs.*
>
> LEN *keeps dancing. And then gradually becomes more and more self-conscious. And then stops, disappointed. He turns off the hi-fi.*
>
> (*Getting the last of his breath back.*) Balls to you, then.

JEN. Mice are back.

LEN. Not our problem any more. Live and let live, I say.

JEN. Suppose.

LEN. Biding their time, the cunning little fuckers. Guerilla war, Jen.

> (*Making this up as he's going along.*) I reckon all the hills round here, right, probably *full* of their secret tunnels and that, like fucking mice Vietcong. Tunnel rats. Ho Chi Minh City, baby.
>
> (*Mimes crawling through a tunnel.*) You'll see a flash of the binoculars, then bosh – nothing. Down the fucking hatch.

Gone. And literally, the moment those cunts saw the 'Sold' sign – back like a shot.

JEN (*wearily*). What the fuck are you talking about, Len?

LEN. I bet they were totally like –

(*Kung-fu voice*.) 'The human warriors they *gone*. Tonight we party real *good*!'

JEN. Totally.

LEN. We won the battle, but the vermin always win the war. It's just life.

JEN. Totally.

Pause. LEN *looks at* JEN *with a broad smile*.

LEN. We've done a fucking good job, Jen. Packing.

JEN (*feeling one of her shoulders*). So. Tired.

LEN (*gestures around the room*). Just this room to do, then boom! Rest of the house is absolutely immaculate.

JEN *sits down on one of the chairs. Despondent.*

JEN. I'm literally never going to go to Yorkshire, realistically, am I? To visit Mum? Like once a year or something.

LEN. When I'm shitted I always manage to call Halifax *Hafilax* by mistake, like it was some kind of bowel medicine:

(*Comic Yorkshire accent*.) '*Guts ache, lad? Get some of this Hafilax down ya – you'll be shitting through the eye of a needle in no time.*'

JEN. I know. Always used to make me laugh when I was younger, that.

LEN. I've never done that joke before, have I?

JEN. Only like one million billion times.

LEN. No fucking way.

JEN. Whatever.

Pause.

LEN. We used to laugh, didn't we?

JEN. Yeah.

LEN. I used to love coming over, playing with you.

JEN. Me too.

LEN. Gave you your first fag, didn't I?

JEN. Yeah. Thanks for that.

LEN. First drink too.

JEN. Babycham. My fifth birthday party.

LEN. It's what an uncle's for, isn't it?

JEN. Not traditionally, no.

LEN. Ah well.

JEN. When I was growing up, Len, you were always my – *hero* isn't the wrong word – *antihero*?

LEN. I'll take that.

JEN. Everybody else was just so – sensible and boring. And you were so –

LEN. Fun?

JEN. Terrifyingly unstable.

LEN. I'll take that too.

JEN. But I had fun.

LEN. Me too.

JEN. Remember when you stole that ice-cream van, when I was seven?

LEN. I didn't steal it, Jen. Luigi lent it to me – well, there were some *minor* misunderstandings –

JEN. And we drove through the village, giving everybody free ice cream.

LEN. Yeah.

JEN. That was great, that.

LEN. You've not lived till you've done a police chase in an ice-cream van.

JEN. Mental.

LEN (*with pride*). No charges ever brought, mate.

JEN. So many of your stories end like that, don't they, Len?

LEN. Yeah.

Pause.

JEN. This house – gone.

LEN. Yeah.

JEN. Yeah.

Pause.

LEN (*with a tinge of very well-hidden bitterness*). At least your mum's got somewhere to go. That's the main thing.

JEN. Yeah.

LEN. And you'll be alright for somewhere to live, after you finish uni?

JEN (*trying to reassure him*). Yeah. Course.

JEN takes out the bubble wrap. Inside the boxes are some ornaments, including the (now visibly repaired) Virgin Mary, still unwrapped. Wankycat is already wrapped.

Mind if I do this here? Keep you company?

LEN. Course not, mate. I was going mental here on me own, to be honest. That's why I was all like – (*Mimes 'dancing'.*) I just – bit of cheering up.

JEN. Yeah.

Pause.

LEN. I always thought it was endless. His money. I can't believe –

JEN. Legal fees. Death duties.

LEN. But he was fucking minted.

JEN. Well, here we are, though, aren't we?

LEN. Yeah.

Pause.

JEN. It's actually as bad for us as it was for him, isn't it? If not worse.

LEN. No, I don't think it is, no.

JEN. It's us that's got to clear up all his fucking mess and – I'm sorry, I'm sorry.

LEN. No, mate, you're right.

Pause. Working.

JEN *is thinking whether to tell* LEN *something.*

JEN. I read them, you know. Dad's diaries.

LEN *stops what he's doing.*

LEN. I *told* you, mate –

Pause.

(*Interest piqued.*) And?

JEN. There was absolutely nothing specific about, you know –

Pause.

I kind of don't know what to think.

LEN. If there's nothing in the diaries, mate, then maybe he didn't do it, mate. Maybe he fucking didn't –

JEN. But then I suppose that's not like *conclusive* or anything. It's not like Hitler's diary is all like 'woke up, tennis with Goering, chicken chimichanga lunch, gassed a million Jews, LOL', is it?

LEN. No, I suppose not.

JEN (*thinking on her feet*). But there's a lot in there that Dad never told me – that I can't imagine he'd want people to know about –

LEN. Everybody's got their private shit, Jen.

JEN (*opinion evolving all the time*). He mentions the names of loads of girls, and guys, and I think it's like he's slept with them, if you read between the lines – I mean, it's quite obvious sometimes – and he clearly treats them a bit like – a bit badly, you know?

LEN. What do you mean?

JEN. He kind of treats them – he belittles them, just throws them away when he's bored and –

LEN. It's just a diary, you know –

JEN. And it's weird how they're all like so young.

Pause.

Kind of the age I am now.

LEN. Mate, literally *everybody* fancies nineteen-year-old girls, mate – it's just – I don't think I have to explain –

(*Points to her.*) I mean look at the state of – all pert and shit –

(*Realises what he's said.*) Sorry –

JEN. Wow.

LEN. No, I – it's just lust – especially *male* lust – is often a bit – you know, minging – and – you know…

JEN. I don't think 'everybody' fancies nineteen-year-old girls, do they?

LEN. Yeah they do –

JEN. Do you, Len?

LEN (*looks at* JEN *for perhaps slightly longer than absolutely necessary*). No. No of course not.

JEN. You see?

LEN. I suppose.

JEN. And what's worse – they were all, like, *vulnerable* – sixth-form work-experience kids, unpaid production assistants, the girls who wait outside the TV studios for signatures, young guys who've not entirely come out yet –

LEN. I think it's fairly common, that sort of –

JEN. It's fucking rough, that's what it is.

LEN. It's just –

JEN. But, you know, there's nothing at all violent or mean or anything, so I –

LEN. I don't think he was ever like that – violent –

JEN. And every other line is just the most excruciating self-disgust, saying how he's got to like basically *atone* for all the unspecified evil shit he's done in his life.

(*Shakes her head.*) There was always this guilt, rotting him away.

LEN. Yeah.

Pause.

JEN. Well, I suppose if he did fucking do it – at least – you know, he felt fucking shit about it.

LEN. Yeah.

JEN. At least it *mattered* to him. Made him feel guilty.

LEN. Jen.

JEN. And, well, it turns out he was actually nothing like the man I thought he was. Inside.

(*Thinks.*) It's not like I hate him or anything – ridiculous. It's just I didn't actually *know* him.

(*Euphemistically.*) Which is a shame.

LEN. Jen.

JEN. But even if he'd actually done it – you know? Even if twenty-five years ago he'd actually done – you know – that sort of shit to all those people, and he'd been sent to prison, we'd have got through it.

(*Trying to reassure herself.*) As a family, right, we'd have got through it. Wouldn't we?

LEN. Course.

JEN. We'd have forgiven him. Moved on.

LEN. Course.

JEN. I *would* have forgiven him, wouldn't I?

> *Pause.*

> He pretty much definitely did it, didn't he?

LEN. Jen.

JEN. Why would you kill yourself if you were innocent? You just wouldn't, would you?

LEN. Jen. His career was pretty much over, whichever way the trial went. People would always have been talking behind their hands about it, you know – the jokes and shit.

JEN. Yeah.

> (*Thinks.*) And you're right. What you said. It was twenty-five years back. A lifetime ago. Bit of mercy, bit of forgiveness –

LEN. Yeah.

JEN. He'd stopped being that guy. By the time I knew him.

LEN. Yeah.

JEN. Had he?

LEN (*thinks for a long time, and then, uncertainly*). Yeah.

JEN. Are you sure?

LEN. He was a good guy.

JEN. So many good things he did in his life, Len. To me, to you, all the charity stuff.

> *Pause.*

> You know in the old pictures, the angel with the sword – if they weigh him up in the scales, you know, St Michael – he'll come out good, won't he? There'll be much more in the good side than the bad side.

LEN. Course.

JEN. And you've just got to forgive people, haven't you?

LEN. You have, Jen.

JEN. There's got to be a statute of limitations or –

LEN. That's what I said – before –

JEN. Yeah – yeah.

Pause. Back to their packing.

JEN. You know what? Fuck him.

LEN. Jen.

JEN. Fucking swore to me and Mum that he was innocent. Swore that he hadn't done it.

LEN. He was fucking frightened, Jen.

JEN. Didn't have the fucking balls to tell the truth, did he? And then, when it came down to it, he didn't have the fucking balls to face, you know, *the truth*, either.

LEN. Jen.

JEN. He was a fucking coward, when it came down to it.

LEN. Jen.

JEN. And those ten people. Those ten poor people, that he –

LEN (*becoming angry*). What the fuck do you want me to say, Jen? He was my fucking brother. I fucking loved him.

JEN. And at the moment, I fucking hate him more than I can say –

LEN. *I* don't, Jen –

JEN (*smiles*). But then yesterday I saw his toothbrush in the glass all covered in toothpaste, and I was like – 'Mum's going to go fucking mental at you – '

(*Smiles*.) So I washed it off so he wouldn't get in trouble, and I was like – 'what the fuck does it matter, you're dead, aren't you?' Then I sat on the toilet and just couldn't stop crying, and I was like 'I'd fucking swap everything I'll ever have to see you one more time, you fuck.'

Pause.

You know what the ironic thing is, Len? Growing up I was always comparing myself to him, this fucking *saint* of a man – and I never, ever measured up. Whenever I was fucking something up, which was always, I was always like – 'come on, Jen, what would Dad do here?' You know, like '*what would Jesus do?*'

LEN. Mate – don't.

JEN. But I've gone from living in the shadow of *that* to living in the shadow of a dirty fucking sex case. Which isn't really fair, is it?

LEN. No.

JEN. Because it's fucking cold in the shadows, mate.

Pause. JEN *is thinking.*

(*Suddenly.*) Did Mum know?

LEN. What?

JEN. About the other girls?

LEN. Yeah, I think she did.

JEN. And all the guys as well?

LEN. People just – they just ignore shit sometimes – see what they want to see, you know.

JEN. But in the end it sent her mental, didn't it?

LEN. She was always fucking mental.

JEN. It sent her mental.

LEN. A bit.

JEN. And you, and him, and her, you all carried on the whole ridiculous charade of his saintly innocence just – just what? For my sake?

LEN. It was all a long time ago.

JEN. 'You can't handle the truth', right? Makes me feel a bit like a dick, you know?

LEN. No. He was just trying to – it was because we all fucking love you.

JEN. Yeah. Well – 'cheers'.

She tries to start wrapping up the Virgin Mary in bubble wrap.

(*Suddenly finding this very difficult.*) My whole life I was like this – (*Points to the Virgin Mary in bubble wrap.*) Living my whole life in bubble wrap. But you can't see through bubble wrap, can you? Not clearly. And now I can.

Beat.

And it's actually really fucking shit, to be honest.

LEN *embraces her, awkwardly.*

The embrace lasts a long time. JEN *is crying, silently.*

Very long pause. JEN *is trying to compose herself.*

Len.

(*With great effort.*) Have you got any…

LEN (*searching in his pockets*). Tissues. Yeah.

JEN (*with the tiniest hint of a smile*). Cans, Len. Cans.

(*Trying to compose herself.*) Come on. It's our thing. You and me.

LEN *smiles.*

LEN (*with infinite tenderness*). Thought you'd never ask, gaytard.

He takes out the cans and he cracks them open. JEN *takes hers and has a big swig.*

JEN (*with profound gratitude for everything*). Thanks and stuff.

LEN. That's alright, you – (*With compassion.*) massive crybaby queer.

(*Mock-offended.*) Getting snot stains all over my best fucking jumper, you bender.

The reassertion of the banter is doing them both good. But it's still paper-thin.

JEN (*smiling through tears*). That's your *best* jumper?

LEN. Seriously, Jen, when you get married, I'm wearing this, and a top hat. And shorts. And flip-flops. Bobby fucking dazzler.

JEN (*with a painful smile*). You'll upstage the bride, you know?

LEN. I should fucking hope not – don't want your dirty bastard of a groom trying to take crotch shots up *my* fucking bits, do I?

(*With a shrug.*) I mean, I'd do anything for love, but I won't do that, you massive fucking twisted pervert.

Another silence, but this time a more comfortable one.

JEN. Come on, Len – let's get back to –

LEN. Yeah.

JEN. We've got to get it done today, haven't we?

LEN. No rest and that.

LEN *stands up and returns to taking stuff off the shelf.*

(*Pointing to a bucket of paint.*) Any point keeping this?

JEN. It's been standing there empty for the past twenty years, hasn't it? I can't see that it needs to be taken on a pilgrimage to Hafilax as well.

LEN. Totally. What about this?

JEN. I don't know, Len. Just dump it all in – Mum can sort it out.

LEN. Give her something to do in Hafilax.

JEN. Utterly.

They go back to work. The rhythm of the work gives them peace again.

And when this house is gone –

(*Earnestly.*) I mean we can still, you know, meet up and stuff, right?

LEN. Fucking course, mate. Blates.

JEN. I mean, you can come up and stay with me –

LEN. Your room in uni? It's the size of a gnat's bollock, mate. Where'd I sleep, inside the fucking wardrobe? In a single bed spooning my own niece, like some Norfolk *Mills and Boon* novel?

They both acknowledge the horror of this image.

JEN. I suppose – then I can come and stay down at yours, right?

LEN. No, mate. You can't, I'm afraid.

JEN (*hurt*). No, I totally understand – if you want some space – *mate* –

LEN. It's just –

(*Wasn't going to say this, but…*) You know your dad bought me my flat? Turns out it was still registered in his name – which is totally as it should be, since he paid the fucking mortgage. And the bills. Cus I'm, you know, a cunt – but it kinda means that –

JEN. Len.

LEN. So I've sort of got to be out next week, you know?

JEN. Fuck, Len.

(*Angry.*) Mum didn't say anything about it – I mean –

LEN. Your dad was fucking good to me, Jen. You can only be a sponging cunt so long.

JEN. And you've got somewhere sorted out to live, right?

LEN. Yeah, mate. Fucking can't wait. It's going to be fucking gangsta, right?

JEN. Where?

LEN. Oh, you know, I'll be staying with Shaun, you know? Sofa-surfing. Keeping it real.

JEN. I thought you weren't speaking to Shaun?

LEN. We go way back, mate. He's a fucking lad. We'll just fucking sort our shit out and then I'm sure it'll be fine, I mean…

JEN. Len – what are you going to do?

LEN. I'm just not thinking about it, alright?

JEN. You can't 'not think about it'.

LEN. I'll be alright, mate. I'm always fucking alright. Fucking charmed life, me.

JEN. Len – I'm just not going to let you have nowhere to live, alright?

LEN (*firmly*). I'll be alright, okay?

JEN (*seriously*). Let me help, Len. You can't – I'll lend you money – honestly – I'll get a job, leave university.

LEN. I'll be alright.

JEN. Of course you won't be alright.

Pause.

LEN. You know what, Jen? He was always so much fucking better at *everything* than I was – your dad – so fucking triumphantly successful – but then I used to sit with him, sometimes, and have a few cans – and it was so fucking obvious that even though he had fucking *everything* I could possibly dream of having – wife, family, career, all that incredible, amazing shit – he was still a massive despairing fuck-up of a man.

(*Quietly*.) And I was like, if this is what happens when you *win* at living, then fuck that, too.

JEN. Len.

LEN. And I used being fucked or high or hungover as a reason not to do fuck-all – I was always like –

(*Comic drunk voice*.) 'Well, that rules me out of operating heavy fucking machinery for today.'

(*Wistful*.) And then bosh, twenty-five years go by – bit of work on the site that always peters out, bit of vermin work, bit of labouring, driving a van, a million hangovers and fuck-all else has happened. And you look back on your life and it's just like a *wasteland* –

JEN. Len.

LEN. And fuck it, maybe this shit, this 'having to stand on your own feet' shit, will be good for me, you know? Maybe it'll be the making of me, you know?

JEN (*trying to believe it*). Yeah. I'm sure it will be.

LEN. Yeah.

Pause.

You know there's only supposed to be five stages of grief, right? Whatever they are – Denial, Anger, Bargaining… (*Loses track of them.*)

JEN. Depression.

LEN. Yeah. Acceptance. I don't know when any of that shit's supposed to start, Jen, because it's been six months and I still feel like somebody's pushing a fucking tree trunk through my chest, to be honest.

JEN. I know.

LEN. They don't fucking mention the 'fucking tree trunk through your chest' thing in the 'Coping with Suicide' leaflet they give you at the hospital, do they?

JEN. No.

LEN. Fucking *leaflet*. Twats.

Pause. They smile at each other.

JEN. Your father's killed himself. Here's a fucking leaflet.

LEN. Cheers, mate.

JEN. I know.

Pause. Tension ebbing away.

LEN. You know what though, mate? Packing all this shit up –

(*Smiles.*) Fuckloads of happy memories, it turns out.

Pause.

You know what I found a little while ago?

JEN *shakes her head.*

Your dad's silver tray –

JEN (*with a smile*). The stairs one?

LEN. Fuck yeah.

(*With a broad smile as he remembers.*) I can't believe he broke his ankle and everything, I mean –

JEN. Yeah. What was it? Christmas?

LEN. No. Fuck it. Let me tell the cunt. It was summer, when he'd just heard he'd got the BBC chat-show job. He was in a *massive* good mood. And after dinner he just suddenly picked up this silver tray –

(*Smiles in the remembrance.*) And he runs up the stairs, telling us to follow him into the hallway, and he's sitting there on the tray at the top of the stairs, and none of us know what's going on, and he goes...

JEN. 'Tally-ho!'

LEN. And just bombs it down the stairs on the tray. And we're like *what the fuck?* and he's going like a million miles an hour, and –

JEN. He's not going to stop, when he gets to the bottom you can see it on his face he can't stop –

LEN. And so your mum, right –

JEN. Opens the front door –

LEN. And he just zooms out of the front door into the night –

JEN. And we hear this crashing sound, and we all run out to find him, but we can't because it's pitch dark.

LEN. And I grab a torch, and there he is, wrapped around a tree at the bottom of the garden, and your mum's worried that he's hurt himself, and angry, and he's just pissing himself laughing, like he's the happiest he's ever been.

JEN. And Mum's shouting at him, and he's just lying there, staring at the stars, hysterical, with his ankle all over the place, but he doesn't give a shit.

LEN. And he's like 'I'm calling this *Stairway to Devon.*'

JEN. Worst pun in the whole world.

LEN. Fucking awesome bastard.

JEN (*tenderly*). That's how I always want to remember him, you know.

LEN. Me too.

Another long pause where they go back to work.

You know what, mate? I *am* going to sort my shit out. As of this very second I'm giving all this crap up –

(*Lifts up his can.*) Become –

(*Thinks for the word.*) *Sensible.* Teetotal. Responsible. Really I am.

JEN. Yes, of course you are.

LEN. And next time you come down, in a month or so, you won't recognise me.

JEN. I hope to God you don't change too much and stuff. I'm quite fond of the current Len, you know?

LEN. Fuck off, right. I'm going to turn my shit around, you know? Cut out the booze, get a job, find a suitable bird, have a family, even – fuck it, end up with a knighthood and stuff, just like your dad. And a Nobel Prize and all. I mean it, Jen. This time I really do.

JEN. Great.

Pause.

LEN. Fuck this shit. Let's have another can. I always keep some spare ones in that drawer in case I start talking even more shit than usual.

He gets two more cans.

JEN *looks at him questioningly.*

JEN. I thought you were giving up the booze?

LEN. Fuck's sake, mate – no need to be a fucking Nazi about it.

(*Cracks open his can.*) Tomorrow, mate. Tomorrow.

JEN (*cracks open her can*). Tomorrow.

They tap their cans together.

A long pause.

LEN (*suddenly excited*). Fuck, though – you know what I massively reckon we should do now?

Suddenly to black.

The End.

A Nick Hern Book

Cans first published in Great Britain in 2014 as a paperback original by Nick Hern Books Limited, The Glasshouse, 49a Goldhawk Road, London W12 8QP, in association with Theatre503, Kuleshov and Etch

Cans copyright © 2014 Stuart Slade

Stuart Slade has asserted his right to be identified as the author of this work

Cover image: Lucy Newman and Neni Almeida at Ivanov Films

Designed and typeset by Nick Hern Books, London
Printed in the UK by Mimeo Ltd, Huntingdon, Cambridgeshire PE29 6XX

A CIP catalogue record for this book is available from the British Library

ISBN 978 1 84842 471 5